A Chinese Kid Named Santiago

Contemplative Poetry about Zen and the Universe

e-Lightened Minds

The Power of People

To order additional copies of this book or for information on other e-lightened literature please contact us at:

614-886-6851 or
regi@e-lightened.com

visit our website at
regiadams.com

ISBN 978-0-578-00534-8

The Barrel of the Pen

Not Finished Yet

Beautiful thing, I'll make you sing in the sweetness of night till dawn's early light. The gleam of the chrome had shown bright, from the barrel of the pen, friend of the wise and revolutionary alike.

Take flight as words press the call for action. Lax in the vigilance of will to instill freedom's ring, yet we so hypocritically sing odes to a whimsical reality we have yet to bring.

The Barrel of a Pen

What lies in the promise of another that you will forsake yourself and your family? How could the depths of disbelief be so vast? The potency of my words could never last quite as long as this incomprehensible act. To retract the consequences of such a thing is precluded by the debilitation left in its wake. The hollow emptiness you take as your bounty for dependency can only beget a life of shadow and echo.

The charade of authenticity will forever be interrupted by the pleas of the invisible. Reprehensible actions of negligence derived from the drive to imitate, relegate the indigenous to venomous status. The apparatus of slavery is built upon fear and distrust. The answer must derive from inside. Freedom's path lies at the feet of those who defy the command of apathy and indifference.

The Master of Ceremony

Verbillary confrontations with pens and tracks, paper and wax. Will you

die for a piece of the pie, or is this the only slice to be had?

Nevertheless, these questions are of no concern.

Master of the spoken word with a deadly combination of adjectives and

verbs.   The sound of your words will not reach morning's light, cause

unsheathed came the pronouns that snatched up you life.

=Musashi

The Assassin's Whisper

Master of the "melodical" and methodical use of words, conveying

spirituality and dualities existence; persistence of the soul amidst the

wrath of Hell's fury.

Master of the split second, to my whims are subjugated the realities of

life and death. Winds of steel, the assassin's whisper, caresses your

spirit, as it returns to the bosom of Nothingness.

The Whimsical Realm of the Artist

It means what it means words

      dance about guided

            only by the universal rhythm.

The sweet nectar of rhetorical inspiration, fruits of the soul bleed into

existence caressing every crevice of thought. The deepest of truths

infused into vibrations and melodic bursts of orgasmic sound creating

life in the dark wombs of the mind.

The Emboldened Champion

Where doth destiny lie, in the cathartic explosions of my pen? My mind's eye sees the prize in which I strive. I must resist the tides of boredom and fashion. Enough about you, see through the distraction, gain traction on the cherished dreams and wishes in your life. Rely upon the real and vivid. The auction of truth for shadows must end.

Befriend the mettle that served champions of times past, outlast the pursuit of critical skepticism and the decorated pessimism of the "realist". Resist the slow death of conformity. Heroically face the tremendous unknown in a clash of will and grit. A destiny befit only for the spiritual warrior, the emboldened champion.

Think About It

Winds of inspiration guide the flow of the words and the pen. Within the rhythmic meanings of the rhetorical, historical proclivities can be discerned. The passion of the people is the fuel that burned uncontrollable.

Illusion and symbols, glaring shadows of fabrication encourage further alienation from what is real.

Distraction and vice entice the collective reasoning of communities the world over. Sober realizations after two campaigns of drunkenness reveal acts of indiscretion. The veil of sound judgment no longer protects the modesty of "we the people".

The Dreamer

It used to feel good; these words flowed from my core and embraced the more. Taking on a life of their own these words sought to transcend the inherent limits of sound and understanding, demanding more of their existence than mere resonance.

Persistent rattling on the soul of the receiver, as undying as the rains of March rattling upon the zinc roofs of Caribbean homes. These words sought to touch humanity's spirit and bring near it just a glimpse of infinity, an affinity for truth lies within us all. We must only claim it for ourselves; it must never be regulated by outside forces or relegated to nothingness by those who fear its seed. Indeed you are powerful beyond all measure. Wake up to your reality.

The Pugilist

I'm too tired to write, but I swear I'll squeeze every last drop of this pen till there is no more ink therein. I'll make it happen baby and set these words ablaze to display the gift that God gave. Pugilistic Penmanship can rip drums and break beats, just as easily as journals and notebook sheets.

The Lady

Athena

Destiny

I see fate in you and if destiny is true, there will always be a strong man right beside you. Through thick and thin in the end, you will realize I tried to be your lover as well as your friend. Now that's real, and soon time will reveal what I feel is true, but yet in still my sugar filled kisses and heart felt wishes are all but nonexistent…at least to you.

Gold Sugar

Late night thoughts and midnight dreams I send to you, in hopes that you realize my intentions are pure and true. I cannot promise eternal bliss, but I often reminisce about our first kiss, and I am grateful the chance I did not miss. Nights filled with passion and days filled with understanding. A heart that is accepting and not too demanding, is what I have to give, for this, one life is meant to live. The smell of your breath in the night, the glisten of your lips in the light, is wearing away at my mind like time, these torrents of emotion I did not expect to find. Candles and Jodeci, passion and poetry are what I see in love's prophecy. I cannot promise you eternal bliss, but I can promise you my heart sealed with a kiss.

A Winsome Song

Good times past, present and the one's to come, a world of

happiness I have found in one. Cherished

memories of the times we shared are kept

next to my heart tenderly cared.

Of our paths if fate should so divide.

Lonely I am not with sweet

memories by my side.

Contemplations Amidst Darkness

Doubts, double guesses and second thoughts plague my trek to see the

Lady Athena.

So through the cold barrel of my pen in the night I exorcise ghosts with

every word that I write.

Pillow Talk

To paint a picture with dreams and wishes diamond thoughts and
cocktail kisses are in my mind and my reality; I can't believe the sight
of satin pageantry in my vision, the division of thought and deed words
that breath I need, in this moment of decision. Reminiscing of flesh
landscapes, closed drapes and hot wax, relax in this time of rhyme and
sweet words. Unheard thoughts revealed, old wounds soothed and
healed, filled with bliss and a heartfelt kiss.

The

Deconstruction

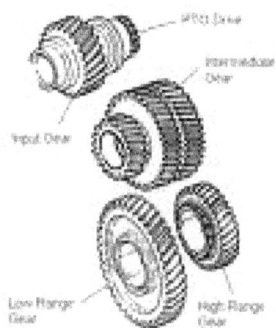

From the Flame

My Soul has been searched.

    My chains are broken.

        My mind is alert and

            My eyes are open.

Desperation

There is not a doctor in the world that can repair a broken spirit. I often

scream aloud, but no one can hear it. Hands tied, feet bound. Desire

cast away never to be found.

Meant to fly, but only can crawl. Created to see the heights but all I see

is the fall…Damn

Take Flight

Bound for greatness and headed for destiny. Satin laced body, reflections of the heavenly. I must remain wise and realize the eternal plan, so that my final destination will be that of the right hand. So here, alone I stand for I am a man. Consciousness from the heavens body forged of the land. My ways are of what melodies are wrote. My days are of what poets quote. Lullaby eyes and ebony skin, kin to romance and to passion a friend.

Contemplative Moods

Sleep is calling me, but the crisp dew of life reminds me of my connection to the larger creation. The subtle chill of the morning invigorates the senses awakening once dormant faculties. The trees seem to speak with the language of chirps and the persistent shrill of crickets. Unseen conversations, which my presence neither disturbs nor deters.

I continue my trek through the earthen impasse and wonderment of the metropolis comprised of earth, wood, leaf and branch. A clearing appears within the gathering of vegetation, and within that space- that pause in nature's symphony, rests a cemetery washed by time. Small concrete slaps is all that is left of virtually a million stories and tales; fears and triumphs, loves lost and gained. All these things recalled back to its basic state…of nothingness. I paused for a second and contemplated my own date with non-existence.

A somber feeling mixed with sullen sadness briefly swept through my core like a breeze over the plains. "That is the cycle of things," I thought feeling a bit of resolve slowly trickle into my spine. Time is a gift, meant to be spent engaging in life, perfecting our work and submitting to the reason of our being. You know that reason for being, you argue it down, explain it away and pretend there are more immediate things for you to do, but what could be more immediate than fulfilling your purpose? I continue my trek...the unseen conversation resumes its discourse in the distance. The morning chill begins to fade slowly giving way to the August heat. I notice the sun's ascension moving higher upon the horizon, I see hints of its movement through the green canvas, which envelops me.

The Way of the Champion

For you see this is the requiem of a champion; I exorcise

    daily in order to reflect the highest of qualities.

        I train by riding "riddims" and battling over beats

            and drums. In flowing over tracks I break

                beats with the best of them and flip scripts

                    with the most dexterous of verbal

                        gymnasts.

Tears of a Clown

They want the façade,

the act,

the one dimensional,

superficial,

adequately stylish version you;

despite the fact

that your soul is being torn apart in the process.

The Essence of Me

The love people seek is one of self-validation. To be loved for one's true essence. To be embraced and appreciated for who we are; the only thing any of us really possess in our existence within the Maelstrom. Economic status and position can all be changed in the blinking of an eye. Love based on these transient entities is an uneasy and anxiety ridden experience. What you love is not me but rather my circumstance.

Learning is Fundamental

Impossibility to transcend perceptions of me, only as large as the concept I see. I shall surely be the expectation so transcend limitation and embrace the elation of knowledge and education.

The transformation of my circumstance begins in my philosophical stance and the concept of "I". The well is not dry in relation to my potential. It's essential to plunge deep into the reservoir of talent and dreams to make seen the pristine nature of my soul, for the whole world to behold.

Acceptance and the Path of Destiny

The beautiful countenance of purpose and reason embrace the path of journeymen engaged in the work of constructing life. The pain is that of birth, the weathering of "be coming's" storm, the clasping of evolution's coattail; bravely enduring the whirlwind. I know not why I have been brought here, to exist at this precise moment.

To witness the passing of pleasure and to withstand the moments of pain; I know not why solitude's caress was chosen for me, amidst illusions of plenty and scenes of felicity. This path's prize is to be found within the depths of the tear and between the flames of anger's heat. This prize lies beneath the surface where others rarely peek.

The gift of passion, the delicate rose of empathy and appreciation is bestowed upon those who seek. To care is not to be weak...to care is not to be weak.

Islands of Ice

One truly does not appreciate the gravity of these words until one is

engulfed by loneliness and despair. The search for the affirmation of

others is so prevalent that our entire existence seems to be based on it.

Self-destruction is not far behind a man or woman with no ties to the

rest of humanity.

One cannot ignore the hole in the soul of a person who is uprooted and

disconnected from the world.

Disconnection creates a painful absence, a void that yearns to be filled.

Defiant

At the end of the road, the path looks bare.

Where am I intended to go?

Is it the death of defeat?

Come and get me!

There is nothing wrong with me.

Wisps of Cloud and Smoke

The illusion of inadequacy stands before me as a defining fallacy constantly tainting tomorrow's reality. The casualty has been dreams, goals and aspirations. Creations of the heart born from the seed of belief, with every difficulty there is relief.

Here I Stand

It is my deepest desire to touch purity in its truest form. Untouched by want and manipulation, unscathed by fear and skepticism, I just want to be. So I must break on through to the other side and never hide from that which I must face. I set the pace to the beat of my own drum. I shall never run from thy kingdom come.

Hypocrisy

Is it not right what I do? How can I demand the perfection in you and

not remain true. Damn this weakness.

Deceitfulness is not the cause of why I stumble.

I am left humbled by my inability to lead you to the other side where

peace and truth resides.

My Life

These words are real that I feel concepts not, but true ultimate realities which pierce deeper than the sharpest spear. Questions of possibilities and fate equate to a deep sense of longing. Longing for that rock of certainty amidst life's torrid sea. Battered by the waves of indecision, submerged by the violent convulsions of time and chance.

This is my life.

The Imprisonment of Security

Concrete—as transparent as glass, build the walls of my confinement.

This place, once a fortress of solitude is nothing more than a prison.

The de- illusion courtesy of me.

The Refusal

I refuse to cast my soul into oblivion for your good pleasure.

Anomalies existence, spirit's persistence breaks through the pavement

of low expectations and vision.

I am the original, the first.

 Look into timeless wisdom to heal thine affliction and become whole

once more.

My existence is not an anomaly.

I am the original…the first.

The Prison of Circumstance

False smiles and dashed hopes, long miles and tight ropes, this one-dimensional reality entraps me, binding me to a "polarodical" existence. I am much more. See the depths of possibility, the rich soil of infinity's desire reside in the concept of "I"; for without this I am helpless.

Contemplation

Lost among a world of passion and possibility, striving to grasp purpose through the fog of weakness. What shall be my fate; disappearance into the obscurity of reality's stream, or a triumphant ascendance into the heavens to grasp destiny's dream? Only time will tell.

The Unreachable

Take it for what it is. Some people want to hate, to relegate others to subhuman status. The apparatus of such a devious deed is pseudo logic and a refusal to see one's own contribution to the muck, mire, and unfilled desires that permeate through one's life. The strife you feel was not caused by my hands.

I refute your stance of non-responsibility and externalization of insecurities which you have deep within your soul. No, I will not represent what you hate, your cowardice leads to a coward's fate. It is easy to dismiss the gut wrenching work of discovery and diligence only to take up the insolence of the weak hearted.

The slope of descent was not started by me, responsibility lies at your feet. Bare the fruits of negligence's weight and take these lessons in stride, as the tide washes away castles built in sand, so will time wash away the lies on which you try to stand. This is the reality, the eventuality of exposure is certain, so close the curtain and exit stage left for what is left is the cold realization that you and truth is all there is.

No intercessors, illusions or excuses can absolve you of this. The decrepit decay and distortion of character will stand unveiled in all its hideous nakedness. I will not represent what you hate and distort my noble gait into anything other than what it is.

Humility

My good is not held by these humble hands,

or plans concocted by the mind of man,

on pillars of strength of unseen dimensions I stand.

My good is not held by these humble hands.

Zen and the Universe

Never Mind that Man behind the Screen

Get at the impetus, the force behind the action, distraction from the true

reason. Treason of the senses leaves the traveler lost among landscapes

of emotion and conjecture, lectures of the heart lead to teachable

moments and pockets of understanding; left standing with none but self

and possibility.

Zen and the Universe

The search for truth is a road of enduring proportions,

persistent yet elusive. Those who claim to have

mastered its secrets are perhaps those

furthest from it. Will I ever really

know? Soul searching solitude and

nights of contemplation are my

companions in search of the

way.

The Heroes of February

Thoughts were my gift heart of a lion, master of the savannah gray

pavements. My domain must expand the world must see truth in all its

painful splendor and unpleasant realities.

Don't you agree?

Now who will walk with me?

Possibility's Reality

The curse of indecision in a world of wisp and cloud, aloud one proclaims the desire to be. See the possibility, rather than the cold disappointment of limitation. Resuscitation of childhood dreams seems to be the remedy for the soul. The key to life is held within the focus and discipline of spiritual mettle. One must not settle for the quick and convenient, for neither can deliver the providence of the

"as yet" and the "not yet" born.

The Bounty of Courage

The defensive struggle for life as unnecessary as the false notions and illusions which inhabit our minds. The sands of time will tell the true depths of our hearts. The struggle for imprisoned security limits the treasure which unfolds; behold the majesty of courage's bounty. The refusal to live and love is no manifestation of bravery, but slavery. Transcend definitions of I, why die to the fraternal nature of humanity. Tragedy and comedy align in the existential pageantry of our reality. Embrace totality with the courage of champions, the determination of martyrs. The race is won by self-starters who refuse to lose "the good they oft might win". Life is on a silver platter, dig in.

Phantoms of the Deep

Just do what you do. As the confines of the mind embrace midnight's sullen silence, plans emerge. The fertile soil of dreams and visions nurtures the birth of another life. Flight of the fearless dreamer! Bewildered by the hesitation of lesser mortals, confinement is its only nemesis.

The slow, debilitating death of conformity, emerges in the minds of the unsuspecting with the grotesque enormity of a mythological creature on a nighttime excursion. The coercion of fear mirrors that which is inside. One must override the binding power of the phantasm with a thousand lives. Strive and transcend. In the end, the sweet nectar of life will nourish your soul; authenticity will be yours to behold.

To Whom It May Concern:

This here is for the meanwhile with courage and guile I will first disperse the thirst of your clouded minds. In time, you will come to realize the rhythm to my rhyme as it slides from the page to the tongue and into the mind. The sign o' the times is that the divine is dead, instead to be replaced with cold thoughts and hearts of lead- the walking dead; men who sold their souls for fashionable clothes and bankrolls.

'Pon the Stone

I sat there on that bench for what seemed like an eternity. In the silence of night and nature I felt engulfed in a sort of primordial darkness, the womb of existence. I have often been told that quiet excursions into the realms of the ascetics were a good thing to do. "Silence is a companion of the wise" or so the saying goes.

Well, as I sat on that stone bench in the silence of night I was hit with no such prophetic experience or insight. Life was still life and I was still me…and that's ok. The gentle light of the street lamp softly illuminated my words. The barrel of my pen gleamed with all shades of sparkling intensity as each word, line, sentence and paragraph was born upon the page. I took a respite from the moment's activity and gazed out into the darkness. "I am trying too hard!" I thought, and perhaps I was. Why can't things just be the way they are and be ok? The compulsive urge to fix, find, enrich, develop, grow, obtain has robbed me of all these things.

There is nothing wrong with the moment; things are as they should be. The moment is all one ever has anyway. The past and future are intangible constructs which technically don't exist, but in our minds. We can only live now, we can only love now. I can't have "do-over" love, to make up for the love I should have gave, but didn't because I just knew I would soon leave now and hang out with future. But future never came, stood me up and hung me out to dry.

Amir warned me about the fickleness of the future. Now was there like now always is; "and perhaps" I thought, "that is why I don't appreciate now, because now is familiar, now is ordinary". Like the night in which I sat amidst its womb and yet had no appreciation of. I gathered my things and proceeded to walk home amidst an orchestra of crickets.

Embrace the Experience

There is beauty in the engagement, in the struggle, in the essence of the

very thing itself. The true rewards are in the pageantry of the thing

itself. Victory and defeat are traitors; do not let them rob you of your

art.

Supreme Ultimate

Outside of the invisible pillars of life and the universe, what shall support me if the skies may fall? All for naught are the efforts of the most capable of men, if first results were not scribed with the universal pen of what is and shall be.

What is reality? Does utility lie in the sun or the shadow? Can anyone bestow happiness upon the broken hearted or the helplessly jaded. Chemically created goodness in a bottle is hardly a substitute for the passionate pursuit of life and understanding, but I am still standing, striving through the night.

No, I will not go without a fight. I will take hold of my passion and dreams and struggle to make them seen, in the stream of time in line with my purpose and destiny. There is no retreat in me, only the calm resolve to absolve myself of mediocrity's decree.

Let it Be

Let the experience be the experience and just that. The commentary and clarification causes confusion and doubt. Deep whole hearted commitment creates, resolve, earnestness and sincerity. For me there is no plan B! Invite "Life" into your life. Everything is a part of it.

Make it Happen

Excellence in whatever you do.

Excellence is what makes all things possible.

Excellence is what turns misfortunes into blessings.

Excellence cannot be contained or confined.

Excellence is what tears down the walls of oppression.

My Fate in Hand

Remember the sound of fate; infiltrate the crown of unbound dreams.

Fear not the decision which leads to struggle and toil. We are where we

should be. Respect the mission. Respect the focus, the locus of control

must be in the Most High and I. Rely on self to transcend the divide

within; surely there is something worth fighting to defend?

Frantic

The scribe sits in contemplation gazing upon the roar of activity and the

mad dash for consumption. Consumers of life's material tokens

frantically scramble to and fro.

"What are we searching for in this endless gathering of things?

Are we searching for happiness, God or a cessation of searching? What

truly brings fulfillment, what truly makes us whole? I may never

know". With a quick glance at his watch the scribe looks back upon the

may lay of humanity with a sigh.

The Long Mile

The long mile…tests of actualization.

Grueling and enduring trials to capture the worth of the self.

Taunted by the daunting task of overcoming limitation. The grim

phantasm - fear is an immortal, with a thousand lives and forms.

For it, resurrection is always just around the next corner… or just

around the next memory of injury.

Contemplation

Is it not the way if it is difficult? Is it not the truth if it is painful? For if

the way is wide and the road easy does this manifest truth? One must

think on these things when weighing the gravity of one's choices.

The Frustrated Warrior

Definitions of me are within me. The limitations of the mind soon become the imprisonment of the body. But I already knew this. "Zentastic" sayings, meditation and word play; I am familiar with the arts, however these walls I am still unable to tear apart.

Live Now

If these words never grace your eyes know that they were written with

the utmost sincerity.

If these words never resonate within your ears know that they were

spoken with the utmost passion.

Things left undone and unsaid grieves us all.

The hour may be late but the time is now.

Shelled and Shocked

May these words be laced with relevancy as they pierce the lifeless shell

of disappointment and shattered dreams. Comatose dreamer when did

life become such a burden?

The Showdown

With the massive presence of warriors marching in pulse—transcending the concerns of life embracing the possibility of death, between the spaces of one's breathe lies infinity. In an instant, an entire lifetime is condensed into a single moment.

The Sweetness of Science

Practitioners of the spectator arts observe sweet candy combinations of

pugilistic penmanship composed on canvases of flesh and sweat.

Solitary soldiers, square circle warriors engage in combat, amidst a

world of cheer and bells.

The Sands

Philosophical leanings and hypothetical denominations, creations of the heart and mind, defines one's remembrance of existence and legacies left in time. Combine talents and sweat to capture a piece of the divine. The sands of time chime the conclusion of all things.

Stay Present, Stay Alive

Effort over outcome, strive and have fun answering the call of one's vision and dream. It may seem at times that fate has passed you by, that is only if you rely on judgments of the mind. Find the wisdom of the heart and make your mark on the landscape of possibility and time.

The Big Bang

One cannot separate from the universal rhythm of life. We are all part

of the process of becoming, cooled by the waves of respite. To do what

you are is your only responsibility. Expression of your nuances should

flow as natural as the changing of the season. Contemplation clutters

the moment's purity.

Manhood

There is nothing wrong with the expression, the role of strength, the blend of energies amidst the endless flow of life and love. Play the part; pursuit of watery graves within the deep is no place of destiny. Tragically this is the choice of many. Men must do the work of men.

I Wanna Talk to Samson

If the attempts must number 102 I will get to you, in order to overcome the apathy that lies behind those eyes. I devise not tactics of destruction, but instruction. Construction of the real inside spheres of prepackaged fabrication. Life can never be defined by the taglines of nations. Relation to each other's humanity supersedes the insanity of transforming everything into a commodity; the oddity of life without meaning, the tragedy of existence without feeling.

Moon in the Stream

The calm silence and tranquility of night softly sweeps the countenance of the scribe deep in contemplation. "If only I could capture a piece of reality's essence between the strokes of the pen. The lines of the page do little to confine existence's whisper, to for a moment stand without delusion to the false promises of desire. What an interesting proposition that would be" thought the scribe. A contented smirk briefly manifests itself. A subtle breeze announces its presence with the soft rustling of pages…

The precision of thoughts continues...

"The division between you and I is an illusion with real consequences. Nihislistic inclination backed by the painful sensation of nothingness, confines the heart in an unnatural state of disinterest and apathy".

The pen of the scribe caresses the page in an effort to give birth to life. The immaculate creation of abstract landscapes seeks new travelers and explorers of its terrain. The pen's emission snugly makes its home between the confines of the page impregnating it with feelings, emotions and truth.

Ancient drums resonate through the once tranquil walls of the neighborhood block, growing louder and louder and disappearing just as suddenly as it appeared. Captivated by the brief respite, the scribe glances back to his notebook. The pages appeared to give off a pink hue in the light of the street lamp, its low hum coming and going like the ocean tide.

The precision continues...

"What is it that we fear, that we would confine ourselves to prisons of isolation? Is it our vulnerability, our morality? Such is our fear that it deludes us to believe that we are actually truly safe in our artificially created fortresses of isolation. This can be no further from the truth.

Isolation of the self confines one in the belly of delusion and fantasy.

This ultimately leads one to dehumanize all who are not accomplices to

its insanity".

A Passing Whim

Savor every moment and instance of life's passionate passing, amassing nothing of relics and idolatrous conceptualizations; creations of the mind that robs us of precious time.   Life can be a torrential down pour or a tranquil beach shore, endure the circumstance-- you can cry or you can dance.

A Walk with Sages

Withdraw to the center of strength from the metal minded, blinded by the passion of the now and the easily attained. The bane of our existence lie in the profane way, our natures' are displayed. What the day may bring is not for us to say, but our duty is to stay true to our way and withstand the sway of fame and fashion, clashing with the weakness found within our chest. A test for even the most committed, submitted sages of peace, who at the very least fight with the passion of many and the courage displayed by but only a few.

Who knew, that with our first gasps of life we would be struggling to maintain our presence ever since. You ask me about justice, and I say it is within. Bend not to the pervasive tides of apathy and calloused sensitivity. Individual responsibility is a powerful thing; one that brings transformation, regardless of location.

Heroes of contemplation and action advance despite the circumstance.

Heroes, enhanced by the pressure that challenge can bring. Leaving the

rest of us remembering their triumphs through the odes, we sing.

Idle Talk and Late

Night Conversations

Wordsmiths

Vulgarity is not needed to stir the soul and move the masses. Spirit
when woven into verbal expression is what touches the bare core.
Words are merely shadows of spirit, vehicles of timeless realities. One
should depend more on the weaving of spirit into one's words in order
to achieve a state of spiritual alchemy.

Stay Awake

In trying to remedy the pain in our souls we often times create deeper

and more painful wounds, becoming the very monsters we abhor.

Thoughtless acts of despair do nothing but increase the source of one's

despair. Within the pain are timeless lessons and spiritual jewels.

There must be method to the madness as well as madness to the method.

On Love

In building real relationships; love, confidence and respect are
important. A belief in people makes the emotion possible. Without
belief in one's fellow man or woman, one's best efforts are for naught.
Instead of feeling a sense of exuberance about the dawning of a new
relationship, one instead feels an uneasy weariness. There is an
inescapable feeling of courting disaster.

Stay True

To compromise rarely signals the demise of fidelity's pain, inflamed
with the mirage of bliss we dismiss the best of us, just for a momentary
taste of illusions' whim. Yet we never win, we continually spin our
wheels in search of a fleeting dream, which no one has ever truly seen,
but claim to have been in its presence once upon a time. I find as
evidence in my life the desire to strongly believe in such a magical
state, to take the pain out of pleasure, the sting out of fate, what a height
I would soar if such a feat were true. I have concluded that all this is
meant to bring one closer to eluding the delusion and embracing the
vital realities in one's life.

The Revolution Will Not be Televised

Look at me in my entirety. I am not one-dimensional. I am complex,
diverse and transcend all boundaries, barriers and definitions. I am not
just fighting for a fair shake or an equal playing field in this world. I
am fighting for something much more monumental than this. I am
fighting for the right to be. The right to be me.

The right to be seen undistorted in the light of history; the right to exist
in the promise of the future.

The right to be acknowledged for the great men and women who
nurtured me and brought me into manhood.

The right to be acknowledged and respected by my global brethren.

The right ultimately to be Human.

The Block

The auction block for souls seems to be just as lucrative as ever. As long as foolish men will eagerly trade the eternal for the transient, souls will continue to be sold. Guns and tobacco have given way to platinum and gold. The lure always changes, but the consequences are still the same. The cure for our pain we hold in our hands, we must not squander it away in the pursuit of pleasure or the aggrandizement of our egos.

The Question

How could you ask someone not to exist, not to be, simply for the benefit of convenience? Beware unchecked arrogance and stupidity.

Straight No Chaser

The superficiality pervading our existence is painful in nature because it creates a sort of meaninglessness to life. A pointless wandering in which there is no rhyme or reason, no grand premise in which to strive. Perseverance through life's trials becomes simply an exercise in endurance and futility.

The Glue of Society

At the very heart of every society or community lies the glue of trust. Trust in family, neighbors, community, government, etc. If this trust is broken, it is almost an impossible feat for it to be retrieved.

Once distrust is introduced into the workings of society than the very glue, which holds that society, family, couple together is broken. Betrayal leaves a path of devastation in its wake. To its victims the capacity to trust, feel, love, believe is severely impaired. Respect and fidelity are not outdated concepts. They can never be outdated for they are the keys to humanity's survival.

Riddle Me This?

Is it possible that the reality of one is greater than that of another? This I do not understand nor fully comprehend.

When misfortune touches one's life, it is as if the sun, moon and elements of the universe corroborated in concert to bring misfortune to one's doorstep. Yet the same misfortune when upon the doorstep of another is just a matter of chance and should be endured with cheer and good humor; how hypocritical a riddle I have yet to unfold.

Do You Eat What You Cook?

The issues are always clearer while in the third person. Forgiveness and piety are easiest when it does not involve the "I". Realistically can you tell me that you passionately embrace the philosophy that you espouse so vehemently? Is this reason enough to condemn others for not subscribing to your ideology?

The Question

I was asked by a Chinese kid named Santiago what do I know about this

thing called life? I know that sh@! can occur. I know that divisions

blur, as well as the people who we thought we were. I know that at a

party's high tide, it's time for the electric slide; I know that nothing is

really known until it's been tried. I know that success is great and

failure many hate, but both are necessary if you are to elevate.

Big Tree, Small Axe

Sometimes in the midst of life, we feel trapped walled off from the rest

of humanity. Why is this? Why in the presence of "many" does the

feeling of drab loneliness prevail? Is it the illusions of wealth and

wonderment that has bewitched our senses?

I have been told that the tranquil pastures of contentment lie within.

The question my friend is how do we reach the comfort of its presence?

This endless struggle has seen many battlefields and casualties of its

violence. Scattered across our soul's horizons lie lifeless entities and

dysfunctional proclivities; scars from epic clashes with reality.

Contentment must prevail. The restless state of searching leaves us too

fatigued to live and to love, but we must not give up.

We must not yield or falter, but must push forward with unbreakable courage within the fog of dust and ash, carried only by the dogged strength of our will and belief in tomorrow. Sorrow, the heavy handed warrior has slain many in his wake. Yet in the center of thischaos we must engage in the struggle of our lives; the struggle for our humanity, the struggle for our authenticity. Out of the cold clutches of doubt and fear, we must pry the essence of our legacies. A duty not to be shunned, but rather the responsibility of a lifetime.

City of

Groves

The Struggle

The struggle of the overnight and the fight for light appreciated the comfort of my previous course but of course comfort lacks lessons of the soul.

So I made a change in my pace and sought change, rearranged the location of my occupation to the city of Groves. Time will tell if a fail in judgment were to blame. However I seek the truth and not the fame. In a market of walls one befalls opportunities to learn and grow, meet your edge again and again, past fear, past delusion.

Fight On

Tired today, the overnight can be grueling—dueling thoughts of inadequacy and ability. I walk this path for me, nonsensical moves are really pleas for self-discovery.

No time to rest, I'll recover in my grave; never shall I be enslaved by the weakness of conviction.

Isolated Confinement

Occupied in the city of walls I discover that mine are self-imposed.

What all must pass before I can embrace the pace of life, whether

pleasure or strife. The winsome ways of lady Athena cause fear in my

heart as I fear we should drift apart. Banished to the night in the city of

Groves, the undertaking begins. Discovery of the self ...Discovery of

birth...

Discovery of fertility and of dreams emerge from the womb of

darkness. To endure the labor of 180 days, in contemplation and prayer

my soul laid bare and willing to embrace life. Whether one sees a wall

or a doorway just maybe unequivocally a matter of perception. The

walls can be a source of insight despite the initial pain of the encounter.

Visions of escape infiltrate la mente.

The Path of Persistence

The trek I undertook from Zaynes village to the city of Groves was an event that bred insight, despite the occasional specter of doubt and concern. I yearn to burn the residue of limitation. Thought patterns of inadequacy I unlearn in the womb of kings. Fate bearing seeds of struggle double my strength as I prepare for the next step.

The Nihilistic Disposition

The pain is real, steel-skinned individuals exist within the depths of the

concrete megalopolis; land of synthetic dreams, paper passions and iron

gods.

Final Words

Much evolution has occurred between the lines and the paragraphs. My life can be found between the margins of this book. I wish you all the best in your quest to actualize personal legends and dreams.

-Regi

www.ingramcontent.com/pod-product-compliance
Lightning Source LLC
Chambersburg PA
CBHW032019040426
42448CB00006B/665